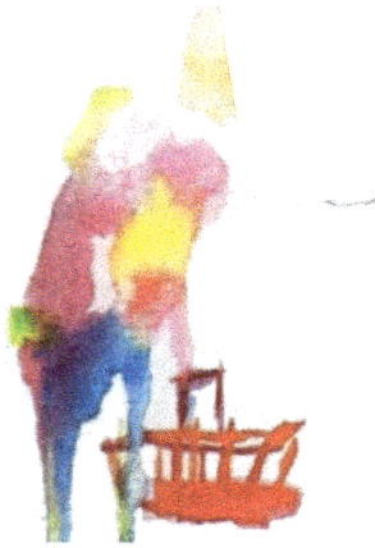

UM

(THINGS I'VE LEARNED ABOUT CREATIVITY & POETRY)

ISBN: 978-0-6454849-3-9
Imprint: Independently published

Illustrations/words: Darby Hudson

'UM' IS THE FOOLS 'OM'
AND CREATIVITY IS BORN
SOMEWHERE BETWEEN
OM AND FOOLISHNESS

INTRODUCTION

I titled this book "UM" because I don't really know. And also, because the word itself gives birth to thoughts and ideas - and this whole book. I usually have to say 100 *Ums* to get one *Ah!*

I've always found it fascinating when an artist talks about the type of pen they use, the kind of blank paper they stare at, or the times they create and don't.

And even though it's part of
their creative process, it also
gives nothing away.

Here too, I give everything
away. And nothing at all.

Some ideas in this book are
contradictory, but creativity
lies in the beauty of paradox.

I hope there's an *Ah!* in here
for you.

With love, Darby.

GETTING READY TO WRITE

SCRAPING THE BOTTOM OF THE BARREL

Sometimes creativity is a process of scraping the dregs from the bottom of the barrel.

And just as you're about to give up, the empty barrel turns into a magician's hat.

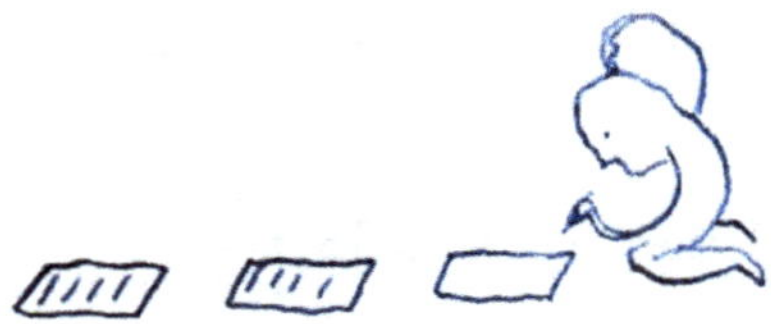

WRITE TOWARDS A FEELING

I begin writing by holding a feeling in my gut.
Not unlike feeling music.
Then I try and write a bridge across the chasm
of the heart towards that feeling.

Often, I don't make it across.
But sometimes I arrive
with most of the original feeling intact,
existing outside my body as words,
or if I'm lucky, a whole book.

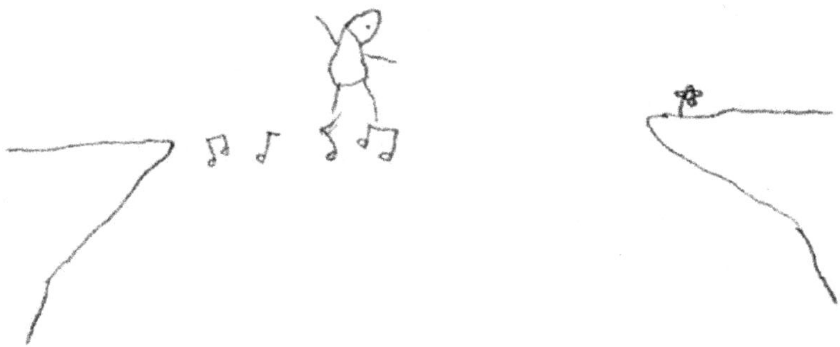

WRITING IS LISTENING

Writing is a form of listening
to the shapeless and
ancient silence
within

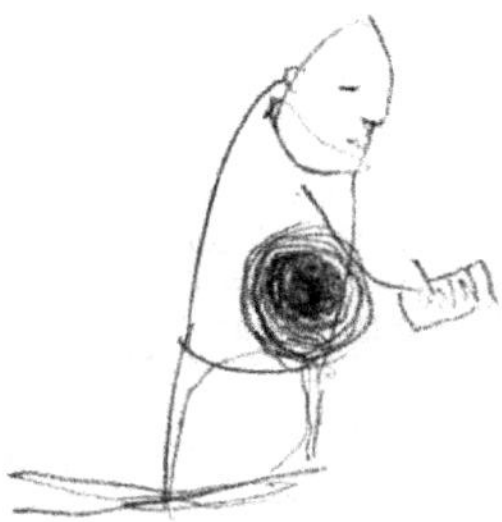

FINDING YOUR VOICE

You don't need to find your "unique creative voice", because the harder life gets, (because it just does), the more your true voice is forced to push through.

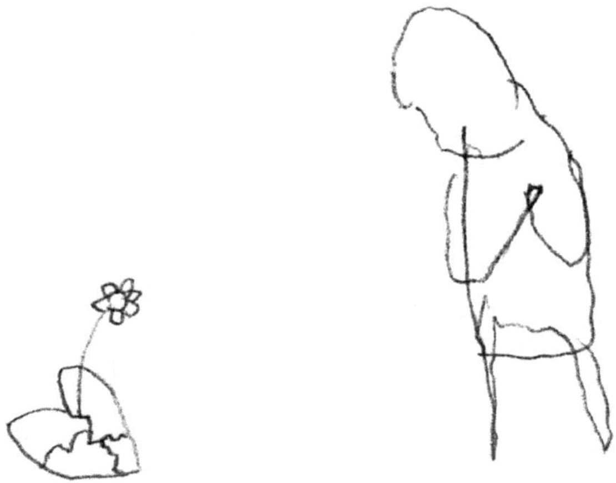

NOTHING'S RIGHT AND NOTHING'S WRONG

Sometimes a fuck up isn't a fuck up:
it's the angel on the shoulder
of the devil
on your
shoulder

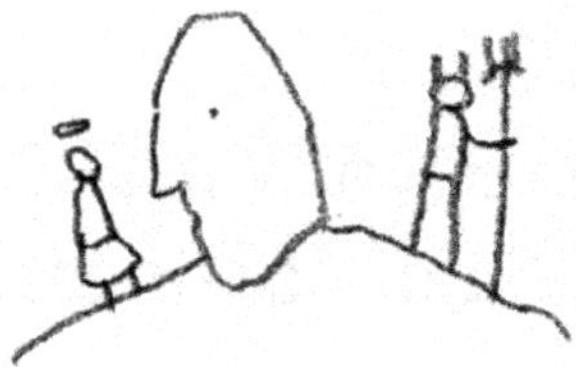

FINDING INSPIRATION

I'll read or listen to people who I have nothing in common with for hours, even if it's to find a sliver of greatness, or something I didn't know.

The 99% of 'wasted time' is always worth it for the 1% of goodness.

I'll listen to interviews with outlaws, murderers, saints, or chat to the plumber who's over to fix my sink. I often find that people who don't consider themselves artists or writers have more interesting things to say.

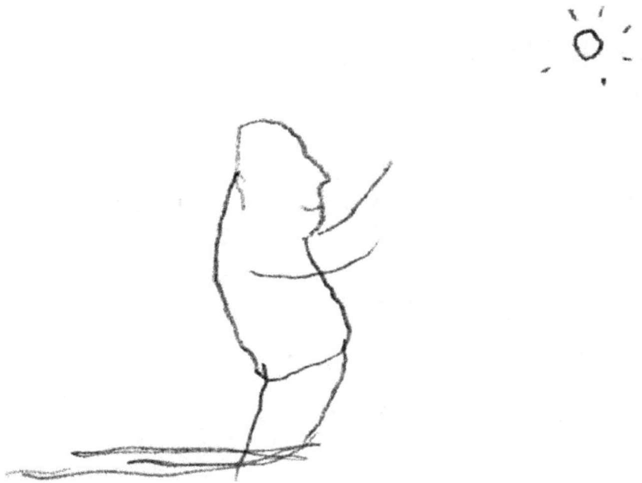

DON'T KNOW YOUR AUDIENCE

"Know your audience",
or "Read the room",
they say.
Instead, wilfully DON'T know your audience.

If you know your audience,
you're doing them a disservice,
and you're no longer making true art.

This is the space where true creative friction
emerges from chaos:
a holy, mistaken engagement.

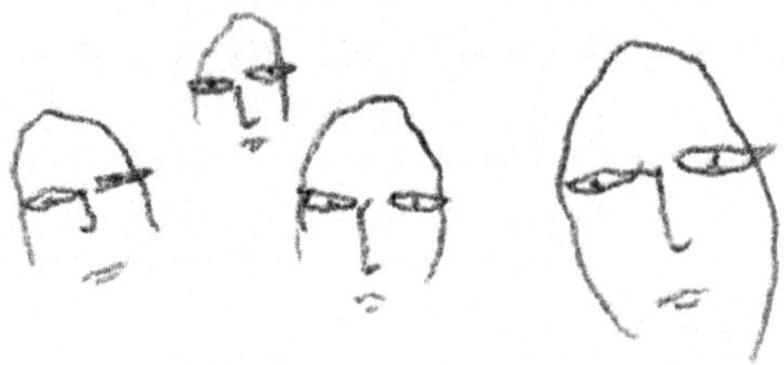

IMPOSTER SYNDROME IS A GIFT

Imposter Syndrome is the greatest gift to an artist.

Because as soon as you think
you know what you're doing,
you're no longer making art.

The best writing is born from
innocent fumbling, happy accidents
and mucking up.

Kids don't know what they're doing. And they make impossibly great stuff.

Imposter syndrome is the gift.
Besides, you're an imposter
by virtue of being born.

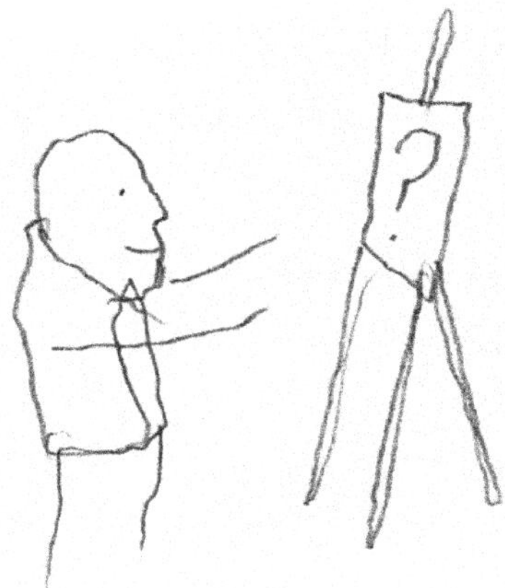

Here's something I made when I was 6. I called it "CIRCLE HOUSE". Maybe the most honest piece of art or words I've ever made. Everything else I've created has felt like an echo from the original source of 'art spirit'.

Perhaps it was a painting of living in mum's womb?

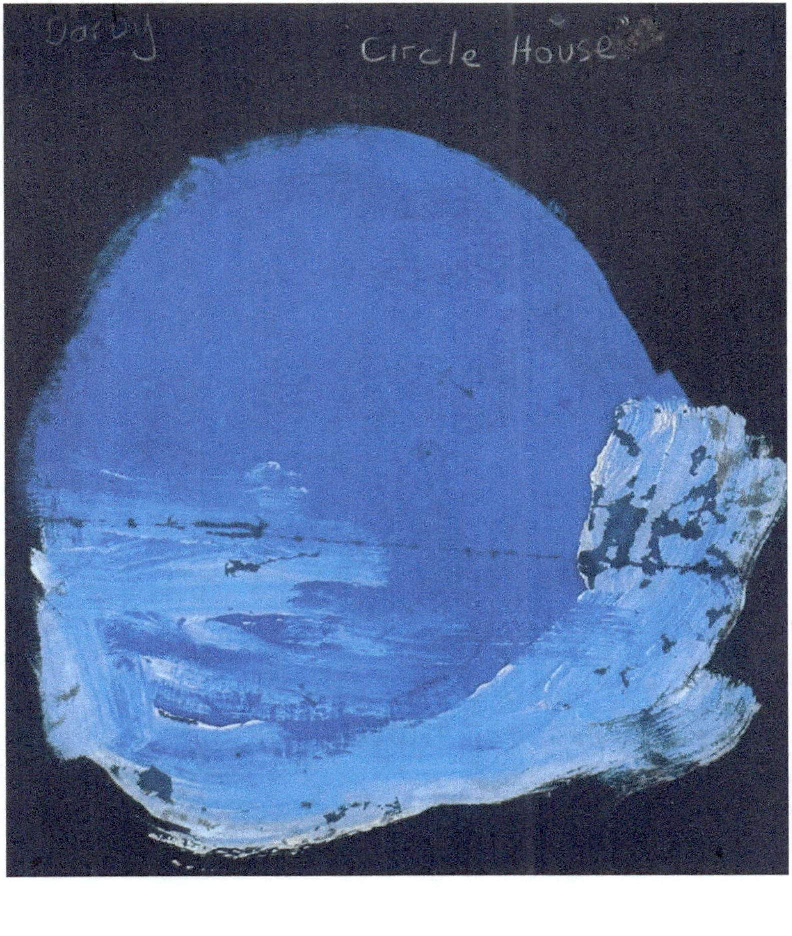
Darby
Circle House

HOW TO CATCH A POEM

You can't write a poem by
setting out to write a poem.

In the same way you can't see
something in the dark
by looking directly at it,

a poem must appear from the side
                                        of your vision

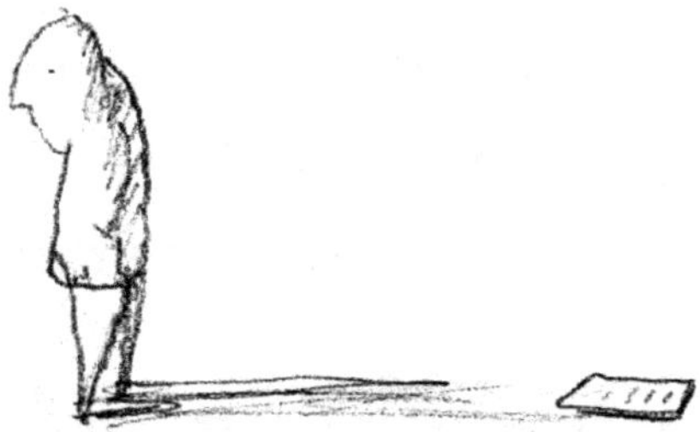

NAIVETY BRINGS VISION

The more I write, the harder it gets.
Now I expect a comfortable arrival, a destination.
And when I write, I'm just waiting to get *there*.
No longer trespassing.
Good writing is a form of trespassing.

The less you know the more you know.
Teach yourself how not to understand,
which is sort of an understanding.

The first few poems I wrote in 2011 placed in the Best Australian Poems in 2012, and 2013 – and it wasn't beginners' luck, rather, it was because **I didn't know what I was doing.**

But now I know what I'm doing,
and to me, that magic can be harder to reach for
and sometimes lost.

Now, because I've been doing this for a long time,
I often feel like I'm pulling levers and pushing
buttons with an expected outcome.

The more I "know what I'm doing",
the harder I must dig.

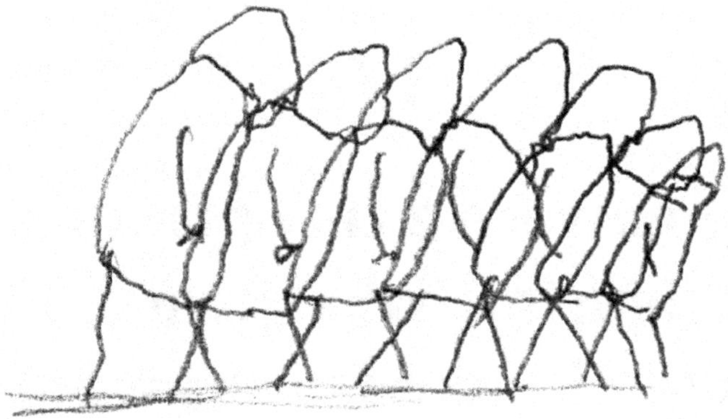

LET'S PLAY!

If you were a tiny plastic figurine, what two tiny plastic accessories would you come with?

(If you got caught up in plastic polluting the world, you're not playing yet.)

(If you thought, "A wallet and a mobile phone", you're nearly there...)

IF YOU THOUGHT ANYTHING ELSE, LET'S PLAY!

NOT TRYING IS HARD WORK

There are two ways to find poetry.

The first is to sit down and write.

The second is to just go about your day-to-day and notice it:

Just letting it happen.

You might be in a conversation or see something happen on the street.
But to do this you have to almost switch gears, step outside yourself temporarily and notice that it could be useful as an idea.

It's hard to switch between these two frames of mind, between living and placing an 'art frame' around every damned thing!

You might notice and reframe a text you just sent to a friend as a “poem”. Or reframe a thing you just uncarefully said to a friend as a “creative idea”. Or reframe a silly thing you just saw on the street as something worth telling.

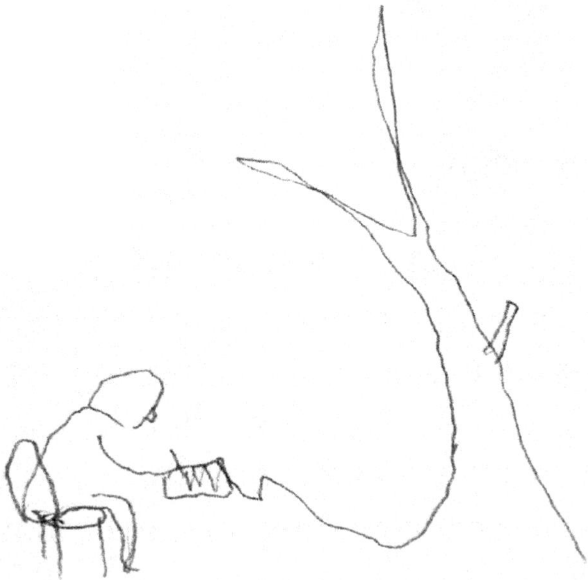

BE A DETECTIVE

Collect clues

As a kid, I'd see a piece of rubbish on the ground and respect it as a clue to something important, the tip of an iceberg to something not of this world. So, I would collect "clues" as a kid, to a mystery I didn't even know that I was trying to solve: a receipt floating on the footpath, a hard-rubbished Christmas card, an empty beer-bottle and a baby's pacifier next to each other in the gutter. A wake of the evidence of life.

*

What I love about the unresolved nature of any mystery is that it presents a series of clues that lead to a vanishing point, where rational thinking can no longer live and true magic is forced to kick in.

Like the point where footprints just stop in the dirt. The point where science no longer has answers. And the artist becomes a tracker into the unknown.

JUMPSTARTING IDEAS: EXPLAIN THINGS SCIENCE CAN'T

Some of my favourite poems explore naturally occurring phenomena,
naturally occurring MAGIC, that no one (and sometimes science) can truly explain. But everyone experiences these things, shrugs their shoulders and moves on.

Sometimes, they're a great place to start daydreaming ideas (for me):

- Dreams
- Hiccups
- Déjà vu
- Scents that take me back to childhood

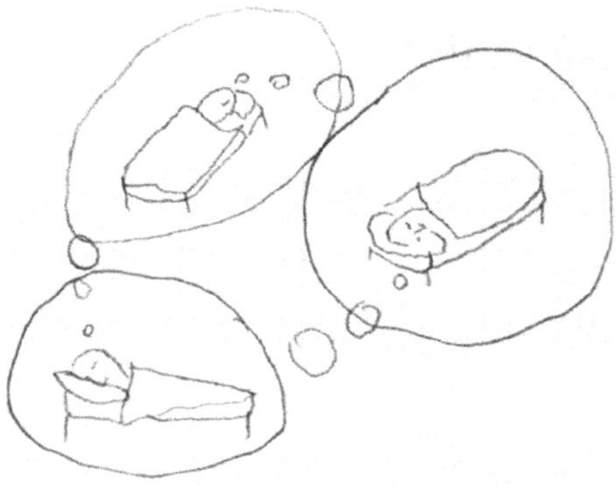

FINDING YOUR VOICE SIMPLY BY LIVING LIFE

Creativity, in a way, is just complex pattern recognition.

The more you exist, the more you inevitably recognise these patterns of the world (consciously and unconsciously).

This pattern recognition (that comes with simply existing) brings conviction to your voice.

In younger, lesser hands, a truth (recognition of a pattern) can arrive unlived, without force, and limp across the page. And readers often unconsciously pay attention to conviction more than the content of words.

True conviction, assuredness, can make a seemingly trite aphorism or simple truth, explode with power.

*

Many editors have said a writer finds a new gear, this conviction, arrive with a fully formed voice (along with a solid and true sense of self) in their mid to late 30s.

Around this age you've witnessed the repeat of the human condition, witnessed the tide, flow and invisible patterns of life, seen humans do the same silly and beautiful things a few time.

So, it's no surprise advertisers spend most of their money aimed at people between 20-35. In your late 30s, you have fewer friends, but truer friends, and you're harder to fool. You know who you are.

This is not to say you can't write something beautiful before a certain age. I'm only talking from my experience and the works of people I've read as – they too – move through life.

I've followed the careers of certain authors and artists who will grasp at the same idea over and over, perfecting it through the decades.
Until it rings with incredible beauty.

*

PS. With absolute conviction, I called this book *Um*.

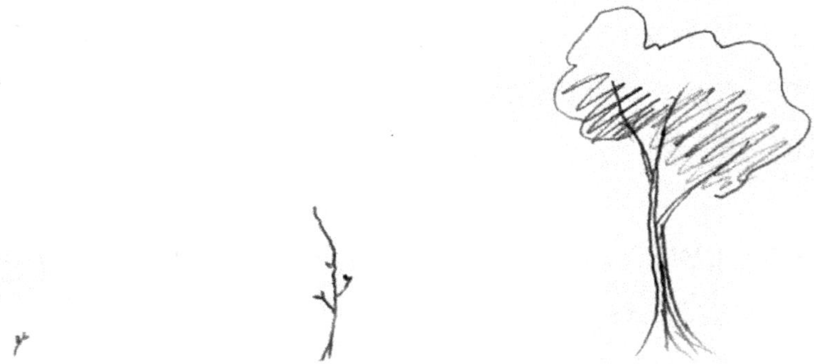

SAY THE OLD THINGS IN A NEW WAY

The truth can't be reinvented.
Truths are ancient.
And every generation needs the exact same message as the generation before.

It's up to you to breathe new life into old truths
with your unique voice
which is part reflection of your heart
and part of the times you live in.

The only thing that makes your work unique
isn't what you say but
how you say it.
Your energy.
Your voice.
The music silently playing
behind your words.

DOING THE WRITING

STARTING ANYTHING TAKES GUTS
KNOWING WHEN TO FINISH TAKES STYLE

I always begin writing by laying down a dumb-simple (but truthful) line, violate the blank page and get things going. Then grow more interesting thoughts from it...

Today I begin by writing:

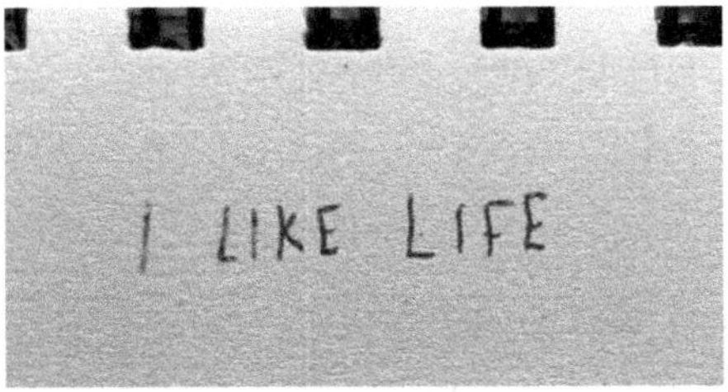

I sit with it for a moment.
Then decide:
That's it. That's the poem. In all its glorious boringness.

Sometimes, when nothing's wrong there's nothing to write. Hurrah!

POSSIBILITY

I need two things to happen when writing:
my hands to write the words and my heart to somehow see possibility in them. And this collusion to become a continual, self-perpetuating process. Until a whole sentence is formed – something from nothing.

It's like blowing wind from my mouth into the sails of the boat I sit in.

And against all
science and logic,
arriving in some
faraway land.

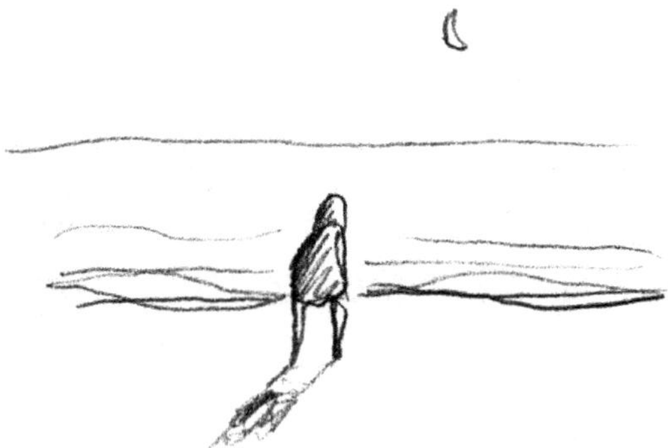

ANCHOR THE READER

When I read a poem that starts with common everyday things, grounded in nouns: birds, trees, moon, it feels like a welcome mat.
I'm not disorientated. We're on the same page. And now my brain is ready to fully engage. And my mind then gives permission for the poem to get a little wilder and weirder.

Otherwise, a poem can just sound like listening to someone's boring dream.

Let life in.

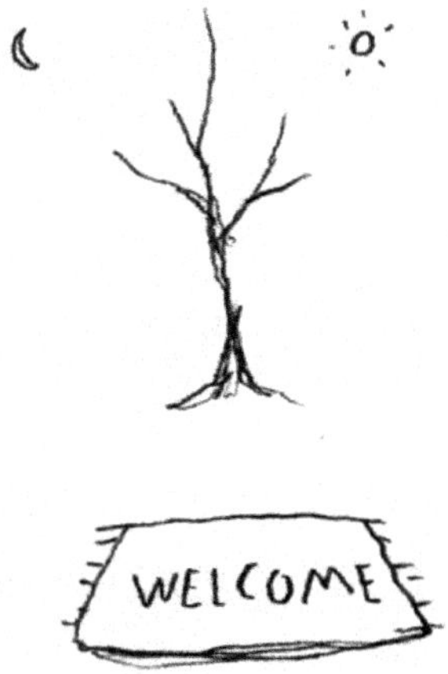
WELCOME

A GREAT POEM IS
AN ESSENCING OF A
BUNCH OF AVERAGE ONES

This might be my favourite thing I've learned.

I'll often write 10 average poems.
And then I'll read back over those poems
at a later point. Perhaps a day later – or a year.

And a single line from each of these poems may leap out and sing more strongly than the rest of the poem.

Then I'll salvage these strong lines from the average poems and place them aside, like pieces of a jigsaw puzzle.

I don't know the picture on the "jigsaw box" until I start testing to see if these more powerful lines, these 'jigsaw pieces', naturally fit together.

Until they form a whole new (much stronger) poem.

FINDING MAGIC BY PLACING TWO SEEMINGLY RANDOM IDEAS TOGETHER

According to Google, a parallax is “a displacement or difference in the apparent position of an object viewed along two different lines of sight”.

Parallax

Sometimes I'll place a paragraph (stanza in poetry)
that sits above another one
which is a completely different idea.
At first, it seems there is no flow.
But the space it creates between the two different ideas
(sometimes)
creates a silent new idea that grows in the audience mind.

Like holding two bits of wire together, and there, the spark!

Larger than the sum of their parts.

A COLLABORATION WITH MYSELF

They say two heads are better than one.
So collaborate with yourself.

Split your head into two by collaborating with your
past self or future self.

Collect ideas that you see through the day, even if you don't see any possibility in them at the time.

Then come back to them as your "future self".
The ideas have been 'baking'.
You may find new possibility in them.
That's how I write many of my poems.
Just collect little thoughts, even if they seem useless at the time.

Some ideas begin as poems and become jokes.
Other ideas start as jokes and turn into poems.

DARK & LIGHT

I like writing something that's wilfully quite dark.
Then sprinkling it with the tiniest bit of light.
And because there's so much darkness,
the light gleams like a star in the night's sky.

Some people will only see the darkness of a
poem
and not the star. That's ok. That's what they see.

In cinematography and art, they have a thing
called the "rule of thirds".

That is: never place a landscape symmetrically in the middle;
always have it near the bottom (or top) of the screen or canvass
as it makes it more interesting to the eye.

I love doing this with poetry and light and dark.
But instead, I'll have 9/10ths darkness, 1/10th light.

Don’t play in the middle.
Play on the edges of the screen, the edges of the heart.
Death wants you alive and life wants you dead and in that space comes poetry.

“If it doesn't concern life and death… It's not interesting,”

- *Author, Cormac McCarthy*

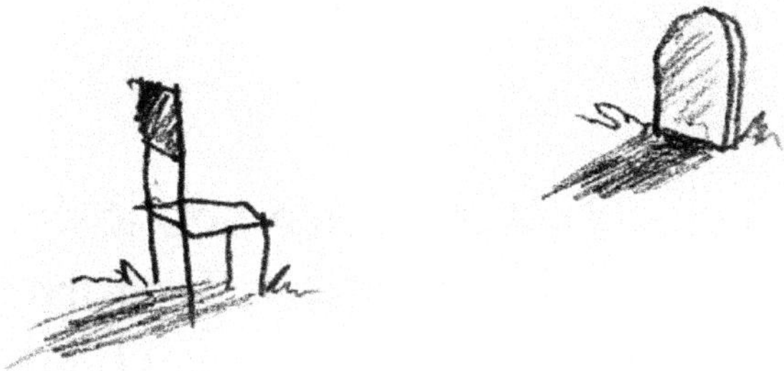

SOMETHING I'VE NOTICED ABOUT ONE OF MY FAVOURITE WRITERS

Charles Bukowski often uses a poetic device commonly referred to as a volta, or turn, in the final stanza... a non-sequitur to end his pieces that serves as a kind of a 'punchline', that has little or nothing to do with what his poem was previously about. It's an abrupt change of direction usually towards subject matter that observes an animal; bird, cats, etc, as a "way out" of the human hell he has previously described – tempering the brutality.

And sometimes these 'punchlines' don't offer a "way out", but a "way back in", a break-and-enter into the hell, only just to laugh in its face with some obnoxiously beautiful observation.

JUMBLING WORDS TO MAKE NEW IDEAS

The Dadaists of the 1920s would cut out words from magazines and pluck two from a hat. Then they'd make ideas from these two unlikely words.

I wrote this poem, 'Who Are You' for my book (on the next page) 100 POINTS OF ID TO PROVE I DON'T EXIST, doing the same thing.

The line – "haunted wig in an empty wheelchair" came from this process. I laughed and laughed when I accidentally placed these words together using a similar process to the Dadaists. You can try too, on page 41.

Who Are You?

You are the florist on the corner of a black-spot intersection
You are vanished smoke in the ancient wood full of night
You are the starless, midnight doorway
You are the dream hidden in the old lady's beard
You are the mathematician who cannot out baffle the sea
You are the breeze beneath the cabin floor.
You are the haunted wig in the empty wheelchair.
You are the cat dragging in a fresh morning.

You are the perfect dream ruined by all the
mornings
You are the fast mountains and the slow birds
You are the pigeons making circle noises
You are the days that rattle softly into the
blackness.
You make me want to go out on a boat and paint
light on a river

An exercise for you to try

Let's find two words that weirdly work together. Find one or two compound words (two words that make one word), and write them down. For instance: "Eye-ball" was invented by Shakespeare.

Instructions:

- Copy and paste a large block of text from anywhere/anything
- Open: www.leaves.glass/
- Drop text into the box
- Under "Choose procedure", select "Shuffle nouns"
- Select "Process"

Now read through the muddled, nonsense sentences and find two words that seem to magically fit together. Put them aside.
I've read hours of this jumbled text and found many combined words that sometimes trigger a line for a poem, or a whole one – like "Who Are You?"

EVOLUTION OF MY POEM: 'DOORS'

One of my most popular poems is called 'Doors'. It's been read at eulogies for people I don't know, included in a Tibetan Monk's textbook in China, and is one of my most shared poems on social media.

To make/write the poem, Doors, I combined the following two ideas.

These drafts are terrible.

But I held onto them for a few years, as I thought they might have something:

1st draft, grasping at the idea, written in 2014:

Go into the song.
Go into the tree.
Go into the cloud.
Go into the blade of grass.
Go into the petal
Go into the fog
Go into the night.
Find and open the door.
It's time to go home.

1st draft of another poem written in 2016:

There is a distant vanishing point where
memory and dream intersect. I will
wait for you here: find me
one day, or in some
impossible
night.

I combined the two previous ideas, a few years later, to become my poem 'Doors' featured in my book FALLING UPWARDS.

There's also an illustrated version of it in CONFETTI TORNADO:

Doors

There is a door in the music;
a door in the cloud;
a door in the eye of a cat;
and they are all connected to the same room.
I will meet you in there
in some improbable dream or
endless night.

Doors, as featured in CONFETTI TORNADO

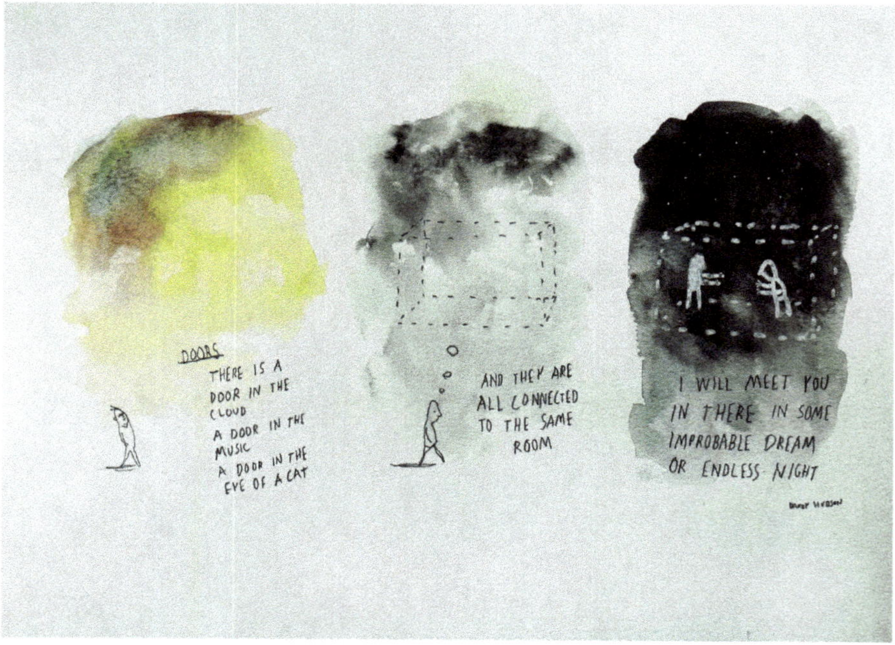

MY FAVOURITE POEMS ARE ADVENTURES

I love not knowing where a poem will lead.

The poem below started as a 'poetic act' when I decided to have a nap in the beautiful Melbourne Cemetery in one of its dilapidated gardens on a spring afternoon. When I got home that night, I thought how silly that was.

So I wrote it down, then added
"Just practicing" and it became a joke.

Dear Diary
Today I had a lovely afternoon nap in the Melbourne Cemetery.
Just practising.

The following poem, 'Broken Door', began as a joke.

Something silly I said to a friend when her door broke.

I said I couldn't fix it, but I could write a poem about it.

Then later (a few weeks later) I thought how silly that thought was, then decided to follow it down a rabbit hole, and it became a "poem":

Broken Door

I cannot fix a broken door.
Despite my dad being an engineer
I am not practical.
I cannot fix a broken door.

Instead it opens and invites the possibility
for me to write a poem about the door's
brokenness and how it makes me feel.

And yet, as I sit here carefully writing about
the broken door, and my unhandy-man feelings,
it's strange to find I've inherited my father's
handwriting; movement passed-down as
measured by pen or pencil
And even more uncanny the curious
bastardisation of my father's font forming

my mother's crazy thoughts across the page.

I cannot fix a broken door,
But I've realised it only takes a small
amount of trouble to set a poem alight.

THOUGHTS ON CREATIVITY

HOW GOOD?

The difference between
improving from being a 5/10 to 9/10
at something
is about the same distance between
9/10 and 10/10.

5,6, 7, 8, 9, **10**

The path from 9 to 10 is the treacherous journey
of true madness –
beyond rules and cultural indoctrination,
the path taken through the
wilderness by night.
To a cliffs edge...

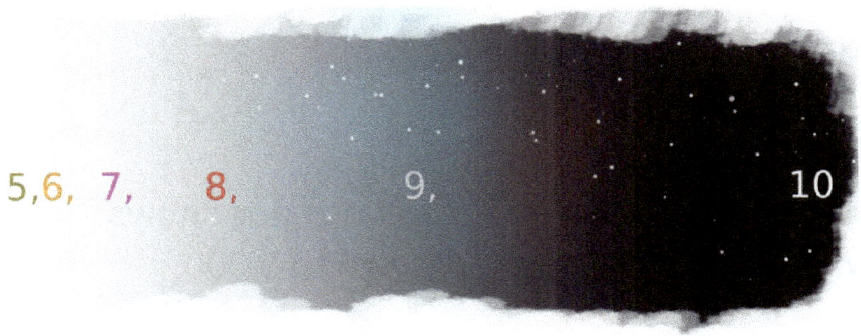

95% OF MY WRITING IS RUBBISH

Nearly everything I write doesn't 'work'.
5% of my writing works.
That's the deal.

I calculated:
to write one of my poetry books
takes 100,000 words – my word doc shows –
which are then whittled down to 5,000.

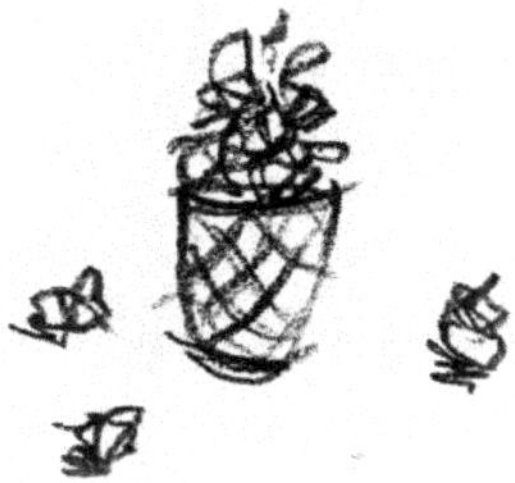

TWO TYPES OF ART

Make art like your livelihood depends on it.

Or your life depends on it.

BE THE GATEKEEPER OF YOUR OWN HEART

A "poetry submission" is just that.
Submissive poetry.
An obedience, a compliance, a giving in,
a shaping your heart to the powers of the day.

So, go where the government grants are not going. Tell the stories that don't have a box to tick on a form. Tell the truth that isn't funded by the establishment.

PLAY THE FOOL

My default thinking is often that of a contrarian - trying to uncover a small truth against the grain of a popular one. It feels beautifully foolish.

I need to read (or write) one simple and small truth a day, that isn't being said, to stay sane, feel, recalibrate the inner heart-compass.

Unsaid truth is hard to come by.

Author, Charles Bukowski once said:

"The masses are always wrong. All you do is reverse the totality of their learning and you have the heaven they're looking for."

SEPARATING TRUE ART FROM THE ARTIST

If true art is 'channelled' from another place,
it doesn't really belong to the artist.

Only art that comes from the ego belongs to the artist. And the audience isn't stupid.
The audience can smell when art is ego
or if art is from that other magical realm.

Therefore, true art isn't really the artist's work.
It's possible to separate true art from the artist.

A DAY IS A SMALL LIFE

Artists sign their work along with the year:
“Darby Hudson 2023”
When it should just be – name and time of day:
“Darby Hudson 2:07am”

THE ART LIFE

An artist endures a midlife crisis their whole life.

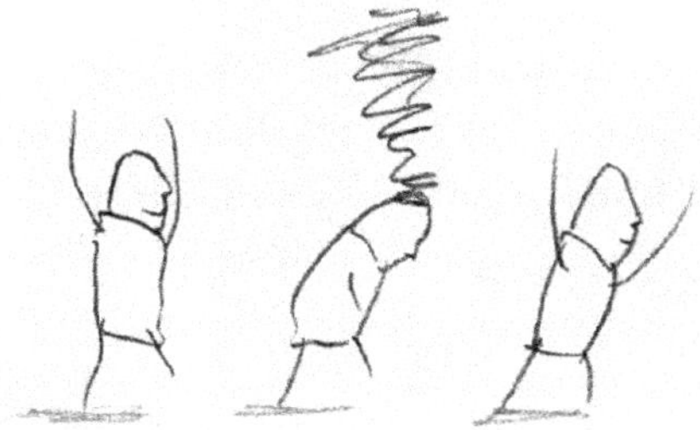

MY CURRENT LIFE PLAN

- Kick yourself out of your life
- Go broke for art

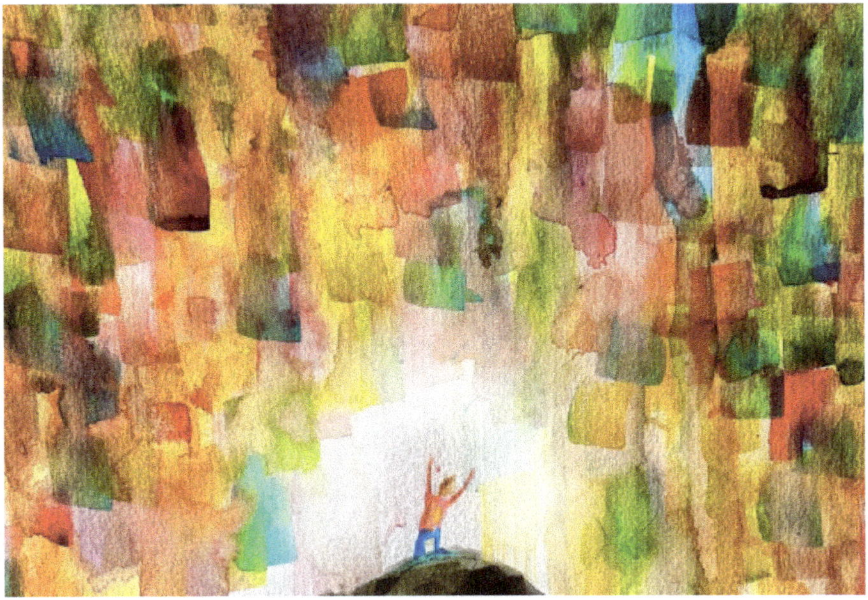

CREATIVITY IS MEDICINE

THE MAGIC OF CREATIVITY LIES IN SHARING

Often when writing, I feel like a sad magician.
I know how the trick was done.

But the magic isn't in the trick, the words.
It's in the eyes of the audience.
And then again, in the writer's borrowed
amazement from the audience's eyes.

Writing's magic comes from being shared.

YOUR STORY ISN'T BORING

Telling your story can be a way of escaping it. Then it becomes an instruction manual to help others survive the same thing.

I often think my own stories (and the stuff of them) are boring.
But when I write them, publish them, sometimes someone will tell me how helpful they are.

What’s boring or self-evident to you
might be a map and compass to a stranger.

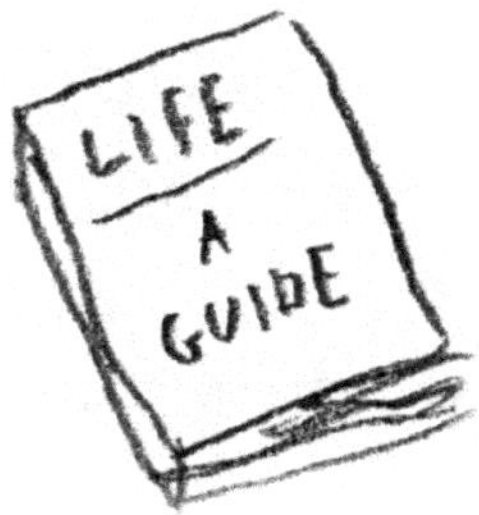

GET READY

When a book,
a piece of art
or music
saves your life,
you're ready to be an artist.

MAKE SOMETHING BEAUTIFUL

...and it will kick away and outlive the trouble it was created in.

NOT FALLING

Money buys you a roof.
Poetry buys you a floor so you don't fall through the nights.

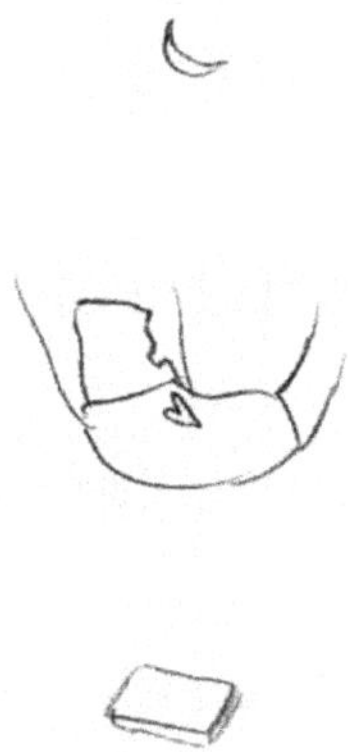

CREATIVITY

Last night I realised Creativity wasn't something
I do to win awards
nor to use as a Key Performance Indicator for a
yearly performance review
or as an indulgence
nor something I do on the side
or to earn money
or an elaborate way of killing time before I die
or for the cultural gatekeepers to accept or reject
or for my soul to divine the uncreated conscience
of humankind,

or for recognition
or for Likes
or optional
or as a vocation
or to dabble with
or for an exhibition
or for fun, or for a laugh
or to make others happy
or for strangers to ponder at a convention
or something to discuss over beers at a pub
it's to keep me from
going completely nuts.

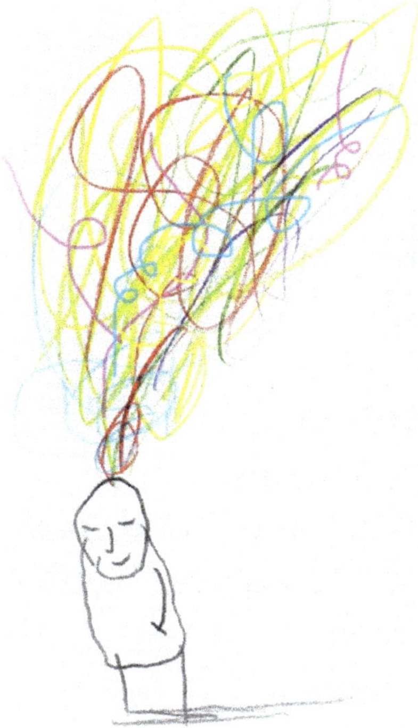

CREATIVITY SAVING ME EARLY ON

The first time I found creativity saving me was when I worked all day at my retail job as a 20-year-old, and my grandfather (who was very business minded) asked me if I was the manager yet?

So I went to work the next day, and REALLY TRIED. "Yes sir, no sir, carry your bags sir" ... And by the end of the day, I was drained of spirit. I felt damned. And I thought, I couldn't do this for the rest of my life?! How the hell was I supposed to get through life doing this forever? So I went to the work toilets and locked myself into a stall, sat on the toilet, wept and despaired.

On the way home that night on a tram, I found a cartoon by Michael Leunig that alleviated the pressure. The cartoon was about a person who felt the heaviness of the world, was lifted from their life into the air and then flew through the skies over the claustrophobic city.

This resonated with me so much. And I thought, wow – a simple cartoon could save me from this world.

Creativity could save me from crying in an office toilet and the pressure of a future I wanted no part of.

For me this was a miracle.

In my 30's, a whole new set of life problems turned up. Sinking further into existence, I felt stuck. But poems saved me.

And the works of Bukowski and Mary Oliver arrived just in time.

And soon, I detected a rich vein of shared truths through all my favourite artists.

They were all saying the same thing in their own way: **"Life's hard, but life's magic."**

ATTEMPTING TO PAY MY BILLS WITH POETRY

In 2008, in my early 30s, I was sent by Centrelink (the Dole) to a résumé writing course. I was indignant, so I wrote a résumé that just listed my interests (most have bush walking) including:

INTERESTS

- Room temperature
- Pushing buttons with really smooth push button action
- Imagining my hair is replaced with my cat's tabby hair (It's just a fantasy, I wouldn't actually work like this)

- Comparing data with completely irrelevant other data
- Getting a little bit wet in the rain then quickly running inside
- Reading The Age in public and the Herald Sun in private
- The enjoyment of being taller than my father
- Lying to my pet, telling it I will be back in one hour when really I intend to be five hours
- Bush walking

I also included "References" at the end of the résumé:

REFERENCES:

(PHOTOGRAPHIC EVIDENCE PROVING I HAVE BEEN OFFERED JOBS ON OTHER OCCASIONS)

IDENTITIES CONCEALED IN ACCORDANCE WITH PRIVACY LAWS)

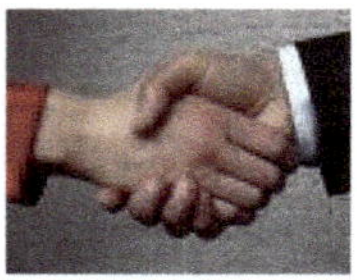

Me shaking hands with an HR consultant from the Job Agency, Hallis, for a data entry position I had just received at Kleffmann and Associates. Notice my handshake (on the right) is calm,

knowledgeable, has attention to detail, and is extremely reliable with a nice protruding cuff.

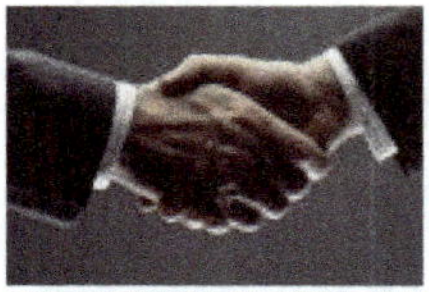

Another job offer I received. Notice how assured my new boss's hand is in passing me the reins – his hand pretty much says "I would trust you with my wife on a Ferris wheel whilst you were both eating ice creams" (my hand on the right). My new boss's protruding veins shows his heart is pumping more blood than usual – a sure physiological indication of excitement that he is employing me.

Then I applied indiscriminately for every single job in The Age newspaper with this résumé over a weekend – 2500 jobs. From engineer to lawyer to bridge-builder.

Employers called me to see if I was serious or crazy, and the truth is I am a little bit crazy – but in the way that I've always treated life as an opportunity to play a long continuous prank on myself – so I end up in interesting places, not expected places.

So, I ended up in advertising because of this résumé. They decided I was a copywriter. I said I wasn't and they said I was and I said I wasn't and they said I was. And so I became a copywriter. My boss asked me what I read. I said I don't read. He said you can't write if you don't read.

So, I read poetry and absolutely loved it. It saved me. And for some reason I thought I'd start writing it too.

And I did that for 10 years sitting by the train tracks at night in the bushes, under the moon, watching trains go past. And in the darkness I'd write poetry as my monitor blinded me, while stealthy foxes tried to steal my backpack beside me. I ended up bringing food for them.

Pay The Bills

While writing my first book of poetry, I still dreamed of paying my bills with art. So my first attempt was to frame my electricity bill as a "piece of artwork", then sell it for the amount owing.

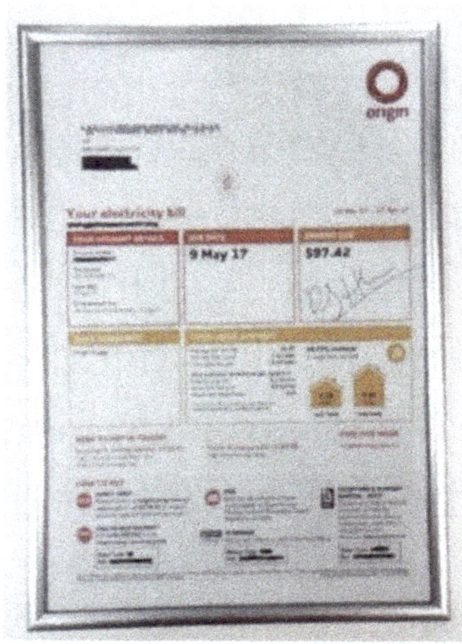

Framed Electricity Bill
Description:

Deluxe framed full-colour Origin Energy bill (limited edition print 1 of 1) is worth every cent of its valuation at $97.42 (which also happens to be precisely the amount due on the bill). It's been in my family for nearly a week and comes framed in a genuine plastic Officeworks silver frame with kick stand for proud display on a flat surface. Visually, the cheeky yellows and reds childishly underplay the adult demands of the due dates while the black numbers speak of homelessness, Satan and are real numbery. It has yet to reach vintage (ie: overdue) so it's still quite a bargain at this price. It comes hand-signed and printed on a photocopier using my genuine fingers to push the button.

ON PUBLISHING

Ditching humour to write poetry

I self-published cartoons and humorous stuff through my 20s. The first bit of money I made from my imagination felt magic. Like it should be laundered by the Tooth Fairy, and not to pay bills. But after a while, humour couldn't say all the things my heart wanted to hear, so as I entered my 30s, I started writing darker stuff. And I turned my jokes and observations into poems, and pretended I was a poet. That's when I began submitting to poetry publications. My humour never left, so I was blending some of the darker elements of poetry with humour.

Submitting my poems to traditional publishers

I began submitting my ‘poems’ to journals and competitions. Some of those poems were accepted by those journals (5% of them I submitted), I came second place in a poetry competition and was a finalist in another – and all these things allowed me to put together a “poetry résumé”.

Submitting a manuscript to a traditional publisher

So, when I submitted my poetry book manuscript to a publisher (a collection of 50 odd poems) to

University of Melbourne's 5 Island Press, they looked favourably on the fact that 1/3rd of my poems in the collection had a history of being published. So they accepted my manuscript and published it.

Traditional publishers take all the money

I didn't want to be a starving artist. And the 'creative economy' was on the rise. The only problem with using a publisher for my first collection (Falling Upwards) was that they took 90% of whatever money I made (a common take from publisher). I wanted to think that poetry could pay for a roof over my head, not just an existential safety net.

Self-publishing and the creative economy

So the next collection of poetry I decided I would self-publish. A professor of English read over my manuscript for my second book of poems and said my aphorisms were world class (I had to look up what an aphorism was) and I was blown away. The professor also said it would be a shame to self-publish my second collection, 100 POINTS OF ID TO PROVE I DON'T EXIST.

This is still the attitude of 'serious' publishers of poetry. I have tremendous respect and love for that sort of poetry. But for me, they're books written by poets and bought by poets.

I wanted to write a book of poems for someone like me – ten years earlier – who didn't give a shit about poetry, until I discovered people like Charles Bukowski, Billy Collins and Mary Oliver, who wrote for humans, not writers.

PEOPLE WHO HAVE INSPIRED ME

I'm an amalgam of my influences. Silences, dreams and other people. These are some of my favourite artists, their work and geographical places who have massively inspired my writing and art.

Sometimes I feel like I'm just a poor rip-off of all my influences.

I think, as an artist, we grow and move from being inspired by other artists, to the original source itself: places/nature.

Michael Leunig, cartoonist/poet

Michael Leunig's work was incredibly important to me as a kid and well into my 20s. He's still an artist who remains daring in the face of a world that seems gutted of wisdom.

Charles Bukowski, poet

Charles Bukowski's work turned up in my early 30s and immediately his words had a force. Each line seemed to count and he said all the things you're not allowed to say. While he's often seen as a bit of a louse and a drunk, his words have incredible insight, bravery and tenderness. He taught me a lot about courage in writing. His Laughing Heart poem is one of my favourite works of all time

Mary Oliver, poet

Mary Oliver is essentially a 'nature poet', but her poem The Journey, stands out to me as a call to be yourself in the face of a world that wants you to submit to the crowd.

Alan Watts, philosopher

I love listening to Alan Watts. His smoker's chuckle, humour and rascal vibe always cheers me up. "Everything matters yet nothing does" is what I always get from him. He explores Eastern philosophy in such a digestible way.

Cormac McCarthy, novelist

The Road, might be my favourite book. Written in almost an 'Old Testament' kind of way. Simple and incredible. Even now I can pick this book up years later and read a page or two - anywhere in the book – and it invites me to see the world new again.

Adam Elliot, filmmaker

Adam Elliot makes beautiful 'claymation' films, or really, beautiful films, that balance great humour and sadness. Harvey Krumpet won an Academy Award back in the early 2000s. A 20 minute film that wakes me up, reminds me of all the beauty in a hard world.

David Lynch, filmmaker/artist

Lynch might be my favourite 'artist'. Less heart than someone like Leunig, Bukowski, Watts, or Elliot, but breaks the wall between reality, dreams and beyond. He is the only artist to give me goosebumps. Twin Peaks is a great TV series. His first feature 'Eraserhead' is also weird and incredible. Funnily, Bukowski said he hated nearly all films. But he LOVED Eraserhead. I love when my favourite artists have crossover. Bukowski and Lynch also met briefly in person, in the 1980s.

Andy Jackson, poet

A great Melbourne (Australia) poet who has that rare thing: highly awarded and incredibly accessible. Lots of tenderness in his work. I've learned a lot from his words.

Mark Tredinnick, poet

Every time I read Mark's work, (Australian poet) I can feel my brain strengthening. His words are deliberate, precise, and full of wonder.

Jon Hopkins, musician

Jon Hopkins – Light Through Veins (song)

I love Jon's electronic bleeps and bloops. I wrote a lot of work to this song that's always triggered a sort of synaesthesia. I hear so many colours when listening to this song.

A FEW OTHER MENTIONS

- **Sierra Adventure** games (from the 1980s – incredible pixel art and text adventures
- **Nic Pizzolatto** (True Detective writer/creator)
- **Nick Cave's** thoughts on life, *The Red Hand Files*
- **Rick Rubin's** ideas, check out his book, *The Creative Act*
- **Terence McKenna** (psychonaut)
- **Cats**

PLACES THAT HAVE INSPIRED ME

- **Dromana** (Victoria, Australia)

- **Train Tracks at night** (Ripponlea, Melbourne, Australia)

- **Melbourne Cemetery garden** (Carlton, Melbourne, Australia): Coordinates: -37.789356,144.966527

All of these places I have written in. I don't really like writing indoors. I like visiting them in my head, too, when I'm unable to visit/frequent them.

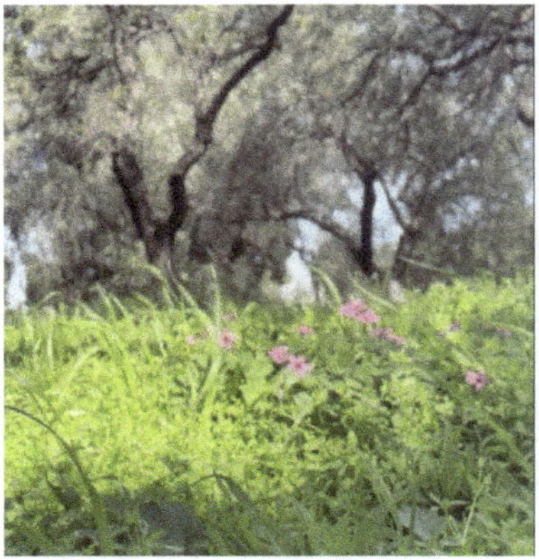

Melbourne Cemetery Garden

Ripponlea Train Tracks

ABOUT

I'm a writer and artist from Melbourne, Australia.

I've guest lectured on creativity at Deakin University Australia,
(3rd Year Communication students) and previously had small features in two books on creativity:

- ***The Right Brain Workout*** by Alex Wadelton (Penguin)
- ***Creative Demons And How To Slay Them*** by Richard Holman (Thames & Hudson)

My work has featured in:

- Best Australian Poems (Black Inc Books)
- Finalist for the Newcastle Poetry Prize
- A Chinese Tibetan Monk's teaching text
- Myer Melbourne Windows
- Inkgroup Greeting Cards
- *Falling Upwards*, my first poetry collection, published by Five Island Press (University of Melbourne)

FIND ME:

- Darbyhudsonart.com
- Blah Di Da podcast
- Instagram @darby_hudson
- Contact me: darbyhudson@gmail.com

Thank You

Thank you Fiz and Jem who picked up a bunch of my mistakes in an early version of this thing and to Fiz for designing the book cover.

Other Books

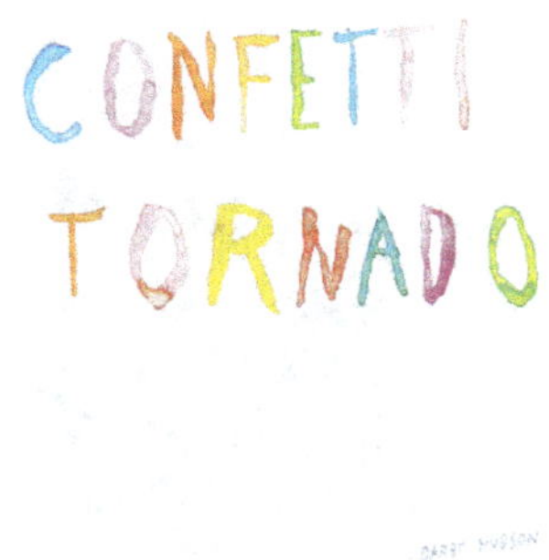

My book of illustrated poems, *CONFETTI TORNADO (2023)*

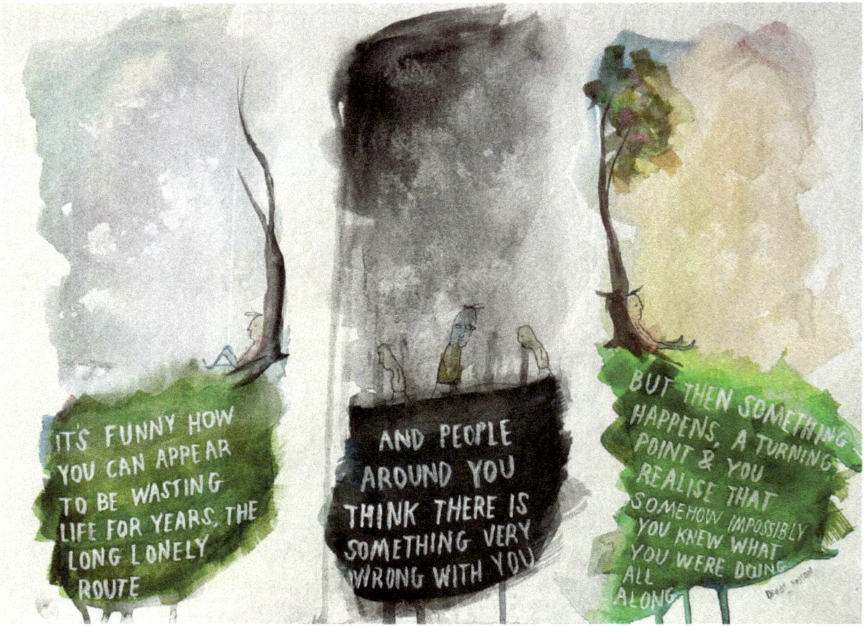
IT'S FUNNY HOW YOU CAN APPEAR TO BE WASTING LIFE FOR YEARS, THE LONG LONELY ROUTE
AND PEOPLE AROUND YOU THINK THERE IS SOMETHING VERY WRONG WITH YOU
BUT THEN SOMETHING HAPPENS, A TURNING POINT & YOU REALISE THAT SOMEHOW IMPOSSIBLY YOU KNEW WHAT YOU WERE DOING ALL ALONG

www.ingramcontent.com/pod-product-compliance
Lightning Source LLC
LaVergne TN
LVHW080543200325
806141LV00015B/537
9780645484939